Living the Mystical Life Today

Living the Mystical Life Today

By

Jim Rosemergy

© Copyright 2015, Jim Rosemergy

All Rights Reserved

No part of this book may be reproduced, stored in a retrieval system, or transmitted by any means, electronic, mechanical, photocopying, recording, or otherwise, without written permission from the author.

ISBN: 978-1-329-65602-4

Other books by Jim Rosemergy

The Watcher
The Gathering
The Third Coming
The Sacred Human
A Recent Revelation
The Transcendent Life
The Quest for Meaning
A Closer Walk With God
The Prayer That God Prays
Even Mystics Have Bills To Pay
A Daily Guide to Spiritual Living
Attaining the Unattainable, The Will of God

Fifth EDITION, Seventh PRINTING
LIVING THE MYSTICAL LIFE TODAY
Copyright 1987. Printed in the United States of America
All rights of this book are reserved.
ISBN 978-1-329-65062-4

For information contact Jim Rosemergy at
jimrosemergy@gmail.com

LIVING THE MYSTICAL LIFE TODAY

is dedicated to all who desire a closer walk with God and who know prayer is the path upon which they shall meet their Creator.

ACKNOWLEDGMENTS

My thanks to Nancy Rosemergy for her editorial assistance and unending support.

CONTENTS

PREFACE		xiii
INTRODUCTION		xv

SECTION ONE

CHAPTER ONE	STAND STILL	3
CHAPTER TWO	BE STILL	9
CHAPTER THREE	SPEAK THE TRUTH	15
CHAPTER FOUR	LEARNING TO WAIT	21
CHAPTER FIVE	LET THERE BE…	25
CHAPTER SIX	TO ACT OR NOT TO ACT? THAT IS THE QUESTION	29
CONCLUSION AND SUMMARY OF THE MYSTICAL PATH		33

SECTION TWO

INTRODUCTION		37
CHAPTER SEVEN	DECISION MAKING	39
CHAPTER EIGHT	HUMAN RELATIONSHIPS	43
CHAPTER NINE	PROSPERITY	47
CHAPTER TEN	HEALING	53
CHAPTER ELEVEN	HOW TO HELP ANOTHER	59
CHAPTER TWELVE	THE SIGN OF THE NEW AGE	65

PREFACE

When the mystical life is considered, it seems natural to think of men and women who withdrew from the world. These cloistered ones found it necessary to say no to the world, so they might say yes to God. For centuries, a few inhabitants of our planet followed this path. By venturing within themselves, they found that life, in all its complexity, is basically simple.

The discoveries of the cloistered life remained in the monasteries and convents, for the people of the world did not desire to awaken from their slumber. However, the principles of the simple life were lived in these centers of prayer, and occasionally a seer, feeling the guidance of Spirit, ventured forth to test the receptivity of humankind or to plant seeds destined to sprout and grow at a later time.

The later time is now.

In silent, unseen ways humankind prepared itself for this age and is now calling for the sunlight and rain that cause the seed of the simple life to sprout and grow. It is now believed the mystical way of life is no longer to be sheltered from the eyes of humankind. It is to be lived in the market place, in the home, and wherever people gather. In the years to come, we shall discover people who are in the world, but not of it. Their lives will be based upon the principles first discovered by those who lived apart from us. It is the way of spiritual things. The discovery is first made in secret, but every human heart knows that this breakthrough opens a threshold through which all shall pass.

You have sensed this opening or you would not be reading this preface. It is more than a preface to a book; it is an invitation to feel the power of Spirit. You see, LIVING THE MYSTICAL LIFE TODAY is a tributary of a mighty river of Spirit flowing into the sea of humanity. Never before in the history of the earth are so many prepared to commit to the simple life. These apprentice mystics are determined to not withdraw from the world, but to draw for the world a picture of the way life can be lived.

No matter where you are in life, know that you are an artist. Each artist sees the image within the mind before it is drawn on the canvas. Let LIVING THE MYSTICAL LIFE TODAY be the image to be painted upon the canvas by you.

INTRODUCTION

This book is in two sections. The first portion outlines principles and practical insights necessary for being in the world, but not of it. As Section One is read, there are exercises assisting the reader in determining his or her relationship to the mystical life and its principles. Essentially, the exercises allow the reader to determine his or her current mystical position. In all walks of life this is called knowing where you are. All explorers agree that unless the traveler knows where he is, he is lost and unable to find his destination even if he knows its name and location.

The second portion of the book directly applies the principles learned to situations human beings face daily. Decision making and healing are considered. The everyday aspect of prosperity and making ends meet is looked at from the viewpoint of the mystical life. And of course, love receives this same treatment, for it is considered our central search.

The experience of LIVING THE MYSTICAL LIFE TODAY changes individual lives, and when enough of us are true to the principles discovered long ago by the cloistered ones, the world will shine in the heavens as the luminous pearl it is. Let LIVING THE MYSTICAL LIFE TODAY be a guide to the fulfillment of the promise of being in the world, but not of it.

SECTION ONE

CHAPTER ONE
STAND STILL

I CANNOT FACE A PROBLEM ON THE LEVEL OF THE PROBLEM.

People notice the cycles of life. There is a tendency for conditions to repeat themselves. History is studied because we believe we can learn from the mistakes of the past and avoid unhealthy cycles. For instance, a woman moves from one unwholesome relationship to another. In the beginning of her involvement with a man, her hopes are high and positive feelings of acceptance and oneness are pleasantly experienced. She looks forward to being with her new companion. Then the relationship sours as he belittles her, and the feelings of acceptance and oneness are replaced by hurt and rejection. This incident is repeated through the course of her life with the only variation being the names of the men.

Another person experiences recurring illness. The inflammation returns after the doctors and patient are convinced the disease is cured. Or maybe a man cannot hold a job any longer than a few months. Always there is something wrong. The boss demeans the employees, or the fellow workers don't want to become friends and are so negative.

These cycles of life are prevalent in human experience. Usually the approach to correcting the situation is to try a little harder or to ask friends, or even God, for advice or help. However, this greater effort, soliciting of insights from friends or pleading with God, does little good. The cycle continues, and it will always continue as long as we fail to understand a principle of the simple life. WE CANNOT FACE A PROBLEM ON THE LEVEL OF THE PROBLEM. WE MUST BE LIFTED INTO ANOTHER STATE OF MIND.

LIFE IS CONSCIOUSNESS

LIFE IS CONSCIOUSNESS is the cornerstone of the mystical life. Simply stated, it means that our understanding of life is the result of our conscious or unconscious beliefs. In fact, these attitudes are the cause of the conditions we experience as life.

For instance, a naval aviator was ordered to attend a school that teaches prisoner of war resistance and evasion. He did not want to go. Many of his friends told him in vivid detail how difficult it was, and that the instructors were looking for someone just like him. His desire to avoid this specialized training intensified, but he had orders. Suddenly, a few days before he was to leave for the training, he got sick and was diagnosed with mononucleosis. He did not have to attend the training and promptly made a fast recovery from the blood disorder.

This strange happening is easily understood when LIFE IS CONSCIOUSNESS. Our beliefs manifest themselves. The naval aviator did not want to attend the resistance and evasion training, however he had orders. He had to attend. Sickness was his only way to avoid the prisoner of war course. His strong desire to remain at home manifested in the only acceptable way he had of avoiding the experience of being a prisoner of war trainee. (Note: He did complete his training at a later date.)

Attitudes and beliefs are not separate from life. They are the windows through which life is viewed, as well as the mother of the adventure called living. This realization is a prerequisite for the mystical life, for it begins with responsibility. Prior to this awareness, life is a matter of accidents and chance. We feel out of control and powerless. We may try to take charge of our lives, but the attempt fails. The loss of peace and self worth is great. Willfulness and anxiety are natural companions to this approach to living.

When LIFE IS CONSCIOUSNESS, a door to the mystical life opens, or at least we are a candidate for the peace that passes understanding and the joy that is full. We understand that life's experiences are the result of states of mind (beliefs and attitudes). Usually, this understanding comes with a sense of guilt. Look what we have done to ourselves. But the punitive feelings pass quickly as an insight follows. (IF LIFE IS THE RESULT OF STATES OF CONSCIOUSNESS, WE CAN CHANGE OUR BELIEFS AND ATTITUDES AND EXPERIENCE LIFE ANEW.)

STAND STILL

Experiencing life anew begins by STANDING STILL. This auspicious beginning is the start of breaking the unwholesome cycles of life. The two words, STAND STILL, (Exodus 14:13 KJV) were initially heard by the Hebrews as they stood with the Red Sea before them and Pharaoh's powerful and seemingly invincible army behind them. The people, feeling trapped, must have thought, we have to do something. This is the usual technique applied by a human being when a problem is encountered. WE HAVE TO ACT; WE HAVE TO DO SOMETHING. Then the guidance comes, STAND STILL.

These two words stress the fact that our first step in solving our problem is to DO NOTHING—no doubt a simple thing to do, or is it? Actually, it is not easy to STAND STILL and do nothing. All our lives we are told to act and solve our problems. "When the going gets tough, the tough get going." "Give it the ol' college try." "Develop the can-do attitude." These energizing words are helpful, but they are not the first step. The first step is to take no step.

The reason for this apparently lazy approach to problem solving is that WE CANNOT FACE THE PROBLEM ON THE LEVEL OF THE PROBLEM. WE MUST BE LIFTED TO ANOTHER STATE OF MIND. Unless this occurs, our actions will come from the same state of consciousness which created the difficulty. In fact, the things accomplished may seem to work at first, but then history repeats itself.

Sean is a man who is attractive to women and attentive to their needs, but his cycle is to quickly fall madly in love. His affection ultimately smothers his woman friend, and she asks for "space." Sean's lack of self worth generates his behavior, and until he changes his attitude about himself, he moves from one relationship to another always having his companion ask for space and discovering space means, "It is over." As the cycle continues, Sean's beliefs about himself become the consciousness from which he acts. Obviously, the things he does only complicate the problem. When he learns to STAND STILL and to follow the remaining steps of the mystical life, his life will change.

Jim Rosemergy

Sean was told to DO NOTHING. The Hebrews trembling between the Red Sea and Pharaoh's army were told to STAND STILL. Your Red Sea requires the same first step.

IN THE SPACE PROVIDED BELOW, DESCRIBE YOUR RED SEA OR THE SITUATION IN YOUR LIFE WHICH REPEATS ITSELF.

RECALL AND WRITE BELOW THE ACTIONS YOU TRIED WHICH YOU HOPED WOULD CHANGE THE SITUATION.

Now realize that the truth, YOU CANNOT FACE THE PROBLEM ON THE LEVEL OF THE PROBLEM, dictates that the first step in your new life is to STAND STILL.

Let us suppose we are in a room containing minute, yet harmful, amounts of radon gas. The human response is, I have to do something about this. We act; we rearrange the furniture or try to seal the room from the earth below and the outside air. Will our actions help us? No, because we remain in the same room. As the analogy unfolds, understand that the room represents a state of consciousness. It is not helpful to rearrange the furniture or protect ourselves from the gas. It is best to leave the room or to rise into another state of mind. This is the mystical approach to life. It is based on the insight that all human maladies are the result of specific attitudes and beliefs. As long as the state of mind persists, the problem remains. And if it does depart, we do not hear its parting refrain, "I shall return." However, by being lifted into another state of consciousness, life is lived anew.

When we have the viewpoint of the tortoise, we see what the tortoise sees. When we fly, we have a grander view and a new perspective of the world we live in. Before we can be lifted to the new vista, there are two truths discovered by the mystics that must be known to us.

THE TREE OF THE KNOWLEDGE OF GOOD AND EVIL

The story of Adam and Eve and the tree of the knowledge of good and evil is a common one learned by children. For most of us, it is history and has little to do with us. Although in some way not understood by us, the act of old is causing us problems today. A mystical view of this allegory reveals a great truth. The tree of the knowledge of good and evil lives today, and its fruit is being "eaten" with as much abandon by modern man as it was by Adam and Eve.

We must not look for the tree in our backyards, in our parks, or even in the supposed location of the Garden of Eden. The tree is symbolic and is, as the story tells, the root (excuse the pun) of our problem. To eat of the tree of the knowledge of good and evil is to label a condition as good or bad. This is the first step we make in walking a path of turmoil and suffering.

In almost all of our dealings with people and in the living of life, we fail to label a condition as IS. It is always good or bad, or some other descriptive term denoting either good or evil.

THINK FOR A MOMENT OF THE PROBLEM FACING YOU IN YOUR LIFE. HAS IT BEEN LABELED? IS ITS NAME EVIL OR BAD, OR DISHEARTING, OR NEGATIVE? BE HONEST. HOW HAVE YOU LABELED YOUR PROBLEM?

COMPLETE THE SENTENCE BELOW.
I HAVE LABELED MY PROBLEM...

Labeling something as good or evil wouldn't be so bad (now I've gone and labeled it) if we did not take the next step. We resist the "evil" thing we have labeled and ignored the strong advice of spiritual giants, RESIST NOT EVIL. The reason we are not to resist is simple. When we resist, we are trying to change the condition. However, the resistance is action stemming from the state of consciousness which caused the problem initially. No wonder our actions are counter productive! No wonder the mystics caution us, RESIST NOT EVIL.

If the mystical approach is to weave itself into our daily lives and into the consciousness of the human family, there are three things to be done. Actually, each of these activities is non-action and a prelude to the second great movement of the mystical mind to be considered in the next chapter.

First, we are to STAND STILL. Secondly, we are to LABEL NOT, or stop eating of the fruit of the tree. Thirdly, we are to RESIST NOT. Steps two and three reinforce the act of STANDING STILL. From this stillness, we are prepared to move to another room or to rise into another state of consciousness where the problem does not exist and where life is fresh and an expression of Spirit.

****

CHAPTER SUMMARY

I BEGIN THE MYSTICAL LIFE BY STANDING STILL BECAUSE I CANNOT FACE A PROBLEM ON THE LEVEL OF THE PROBLEM.

CHAPTER TWO
BE STILL

KNOW GOD

The mystical process is one of being lifted into an awareness of God's presence. Spirit is our sufficiency, and when we are conscious of God, the challenges of life are met. Therefore, the purpose of the simple life is to KNOW GOD. This brings a shocking revelation. The problem is not the issue; our purpose is to be aware of God's presence and power.

In essence, we are moving from a problem oriented existence of pain and hopelessness, through a solution oriented approach to daily living yielding hope, to a God centered life transcending the human position. This is not as easy as it seems. The subtle actions of the pygmy self are coy and effective.

An image illustrates the subtleties of the pygmy self's scheme for "creative" living. Figuratively speaking, God hears we are coming to visit. It is assumed we are coming to get to KNOW HIM, and the Spirit of the universe is excited because finally a relationship will develop with us. The house is cleaned, tea is prepared, and Spirit waits for us. And we come. We arrive dressed in our work clothes, and as God answers the door we ask to borrow the lawn mower, for ours is broken.

This illustration depicts the way we interact with God. There is no desire to form a relationship with Spirit. Instead, we have a need, and we hope God can fulfill it. Of course, usually it is not a lawn mower, but don't rule out the possibility. We ask for help in any situation which concerns us. It is also believed the Almighty is an employment agency and can find us a job, or at least come up with a certain sum of money to help with the rent. If there is a decision to be made, God shows the way. These are human wants and are to be met, but where is the relationship with God? In short, it is non-existent.

Jim Rosemergy

IN THE SPACE PROVIDED BELOW INDICATE YOUR "LAWN MOWER" OR WHAT IT IS YOU HAVE ASKED GOD TO PROVIDE FOR YOU OR TO DO FOR YOU.

I've asked God to let me have dreams that I can remember & interpret. I also asked God to provide me a winning lottery # via my dreams.

In the mystical way of life, the true yearning of the soul is to be acknowledged and ultimately fulfilled. It is a relationship with the Presence, the discovery of what it is to be made in the image and after the likeness of God. This oneness is the focus of life. It comes as the result of a powerful realization. "Seek first the kingdom (an awareness of God/the relationship with Spirit)…and all these things (lawn mowers, jobs, decisions, healings, marriages) shall be yours as well." Matthew 6:33. The mystical life is not setting aside the human dimension of life. It is assigning it its proper place.

This explains why it is written in the Bible, "…your Father knows what you need before you ask him." Matthew 6:8. Many of us believe this means God knows about our disease, or the desire for a marriage. Actually, the statement is based on God knowing our single spiritual need rather than every varied human desire. God knows our every need, for God knows we have but one need, to KNOW HIM. *Her*

The recognition of this idea comes to every spiritual seeker. It cannot be hurried. BEING STILL is required. Did not the psalmist hear the still, small voice declare, "BE STILL, and know that I am God"? Psalm 46:10. This will be discussed further in another chapter, but please realize KNOWING GOD cannot be an act of will. We knock and then must wait for the door to be opened. Even before we attempt to BE STILL, it is necessary to sense the soul's supreme ambition to KNOW GOD.

GOD IS ENOUGH

As we understand this truth, the worldly problem is put aside. It is not the issue. Nor will the problem's resolution appear because of our manipulation of people and conditions. In fact, the solution is an added thing naturally manifesting itself because we are true to KNOWING GOD.

In my life there was a happening which indelibly marked my soul, so this truth and the simple life could no longer be ignored. During the autumn in response to an inner prompting to write, I traveled to a lake cabin in Idaho to be alone. I arrived, built a fire in the fireplace, and set up the computer, so the writing could begin. Two paragraphs were typed, and then suddenly the cursor refused to move. I checked connections and changed programs, but to no avail. Then the pleading began.

"God, you have guided me to come to this place to write. I have been trying to find this time for years and looking forward to the occasion for months, and now the cursor locks up."

The cursor remained in place conveying its silent message. Finally, composure returned, and the dialogue with Spirit continued with my ear now prepared to listen.

I said, "I am here to write. Why is this happening?"

Then an unmistakable voice replied, "Jim, you are not here to write. In all you do, in all your ways, you have but one need, one purpose. It is to KNOW ME." With this realization, my hands once again touched the keyboard, the cursor began to move, and the writing continued.

Such an experience is not forgotten. The purpose of life is forged in the soul by two words, KNOW GOD. No longer is the outer world conformed to human wants and wishes. God is first, and life is ordered. There is no attempt to ask God to do something for us or to bless us with anything other than the Presence. The practice of asking for anything other than the kingdom passes away. What is better than an awareness of God? Isn't life consciousness? What will life be like when its beginning is in God? A simple phrase comes alive. GOD IS ENOUGH. It reinforces the apostle Paul's experience in which he heard, "My grace is sufficient for you..." II Corinthians 12:9.

THE ADDED THINGS

Another image of God comes and builds upon the truth discovered at the lake in Idaho. In this vision, we return home to our house. There is a package, a gift, on the doorstep. It is from our Friend, God. The gift is appreciated, but we are sorry we missed our Friend and were unable to speak and to share with our Friend. The gift represents the healing, the new job, the person who lights up our life, or the lawn

Jim Rosemergy

mower. It is the result of a growing relationship with Spirit; it is the fruit of seeking first the kingdom. The gift is an added thing. We are grateful, but we understand the gift is not what we seek.

The image continues. The next day we enter our house, and the air is filled with a delightful fragrance. We know it is evidence of the Presence of God. It is fresh and illustrates to us we have just missed our Friend. The relationship has become so important to us that it is our aspiration. The fragrance represents feelings of peace and love, and keen insights into the spiritual way of life. These, like the healing, the new job, are appreciated, but our maturity enables us to hold the idea that GOD IS OUR SUFFICIENCY. Positive feelings may be the fragrance or evidence of Spirit, but they are not the "real thing." Remember, the purpose of the simple life is to KNOW GOD, and always and in all our ways, we search for that which is forever with us.

BEING STILL

If our search is to be fruitful, the second major step in the mystical process must be enacted, BE STILL. Method is not important. Motive is the determining factor. Within each of us is the roadmap charting the way to the experience of God's presence. Stated simply, WE COME COMPLETE WITH INSTRUCTIONS. If the desire is pure and the eye is single, all is well.

Perhaps it is best to dedicate ourselves to the life of stillness through a covenant. If you feel comfortable with the covenant below and know your time to make a commitment to Spirit is at hand, sign the agreement and continue to chapter three and the next step in the mystical life.

I feel the movement of Spirit within me. It has quickened a desire to know God above all else. I desire to seek first the kingdom knowing that as I do, all else is added unto me. I do not focus upon the added things, but have the single eye. In my daily prayer life, I ask only to experience the Presence. I adopt this simple life, for I understand God is enough.

Peggy H. Taylor
Signature

Peggy H. Taylor 11/27/22

With the signing of the covenant, you have made BEING STILL a way of life, for to BE STILL is to turn to God as the answer to all of life's challenges. Specific answers are no longer sought. No matter what the problem, it is now acknowledged that there is only one answer—an awareness of God. From this consciousness, life is seen and lived anew.

****

CHAPTER SUMMARY

BY BEING STILL, I BEGIN THE ASCENT TO THE HEIGHT OF GOD'S PRESENCE, AND I DECLARE THAT A CONSCIOUSNESS OF GOD IS ENOUGH.

CHAPTER THREE
SPEAK THE TRUTH

WHAT GOD CAN DO, GOD IS DOING.

The mystical life is a life of prayer, but prayer is not an attempt to have the Almighty do what we want Him to do. It is an expression of our commitment to KNOW GOD. Joel Goldsmith, one who pursued the simple life, uttered a principle which is the foundation of a life of prayer. WHAT GOD CAN DO, GOD IS DOING. An understanding of this idea changes our way of praying.

No longer do we attempt to have God serve us. Imagine a live-in-servant with God's capabilities. Hasn't this been our hope for thousands of years? There is the assumption that God is capable of helping us, but is reluctant to act on our behalf. Perhaps we think we are not spiritual enough, so we promise to be better. If we do not want to go this far, we bargain with the Almighty. "God, I'll do this, if You do…" Our proposals and attempts at motivating God or our lectures pointing out our needs and what God has not done are considered prayer. However, no matter how expert our salesmanship, how appealing our bargain, how logical our argument, Spirit is unmoved, for WHAT GOD CAN DO, GOD IS DOING. And what is God doing?

GOD IS BEING…

GOD IS BEING LIFE, and when this consciousness dawns in us, we realize our wholeness and are healed. GOD IS BEING LOVE, and as this truth makes itself known, we are loved and loving. GOD IS BEING THE SOURCE, and when we know this, we trust. We are secure, and all our tangible needs are met. The list goes on, each pointing to our need not to have God do anything, but for us to rise into an awareness of what GOD IS BEING.

It is a law of life that our consciousness manifests itself as our life experience. Imagine life's experience when we are aware we are expressions of God life (Actually it is beyond imagining). Let us

Jim Rosemergy

imagine, if we can, the quality of our human relationships when we are consciously aware of Divine Love.

This insight serves as another portion of the foundation of the mystical life. Not only does our awareness of Spirit manifest Itself in our daily life, but we act from this consciousness becoming instruments of Spirit.

AN EXAMPLE OF MYSTICAL LIVING TODAY

Our commitment to awakening to GOD'S BEINGNESS leads to non-resistance and a lack of enthusiasm for changing the human condition. The spiritually oriented individual realizes there is no permanent outer change unless inner transformation is the prelude. Years ago during World War II, a couple adopted the simple life. While their neighbors ran to underground shelters during German air raids, the couple watched for fires ignited by the bombing. Devastation was often around them, but they were not harmed. Their neighbors' houses were damaged or destroyed, but their home was untouched.

This is a grand example of the mystical method impacting daily life. The normal human response was to hide in the bomb shelter, but these God centered individuals walked the streets. Their house was untouched because their true dwelling place was the Presence of God. Rather than resist the menace from above by hiding in the shelter below, these trusting and courageous people chose to rise into an awareness of the shelter of the Most High.

In our course of study, we are marching toward this approach to life. We have seen the value of STANDING STILL and purified our motives by BEING STILL. Now it is time for the third major step of the mystical way of life. It is called SPEAKING THE TRUTH.

SPEAK THE TRUTH

A deterrent to experiencing the Presence of God is our five senses. They are our servants, and yet there are times when they are master and king. We try to STAND STILL, but the messages of our senses distract us, and we resist them. Not only is it a matter of our senses, but our thoughts begin to run rampant through our minds, and we are unable to give our attention to awakening to God's presence.

All mystics have learned that the senses, their messages, and unruly thoughts can be friends bringing us closer to a realization of the Presence. They are actually doormen of the kingdom of God, for they bring us to the NOW. The key point is that the kingdom of God is at hand. In it we live and move and have our being. The kingdom is here and now, and if we live in the NOW, we are candidates to KNOW GOD.

The process is as follows. Do not resist the messages of the senses; welcome them. As we are still and declare that our purpose is a relationship with God, we look around us and allow the sense of sight to provide us with an image of our surroundings. We look carefully not only at the obvious, but at the shadows cast by objects and the light reflecting off the surroundings. Then gently we invite the sense of sight to sleep. We close our eyes, but assure our servant that in a short time we shall invite its messages again.

Next, we listen for sounds far and near, for those sounds rude and those which are soft like the silence we desire. To each sound we say, "I do not resist you. You are here as I am." Once our peace is made with the sounds around us, this servant is asked to sleep.

Next, we sense our body temple. We observe the rise and fall of our chest. We note the position of our hands and feet. All of these efforts, including the looking and listening, are bringing us into the Now. In the Now is the Presence of God. This process is continued with fragrances in the air if any are noted and also with any taste we sense.

Finally, our attention is directed inward, and our thoughts are noted. None are resisted or labeled as good or bad. There is no condemnation, only observation. We have become the watcher. Our attention is in the moment, and we are prepared to SPEAK THE TRUTH.

Here is an example of the inner journey you might experience as you become "the Watcher."

I am the watcher, open to the world around me, but always remembering, I am in the world, but not of it. My purpose is to know my God, my dear Friend.

Jim Rosemergy

And so I watch, welcoming the messages of my senses. I see what is to be seen.

Images around me. Objects near and far. Light reflecting off surfaces, deep shadows.

I do not judge or label what I see. I see with the eyes of Spirit.

And then I invite the sense of sight to sleep, and I listen.

For sounds, far and near. Those soft and loud.

Sounds to embrace, sounds that intrude.

All are a part of my world. I take them inside without judgment.

I am the Watcher.

I turn my attention to my body temple.

I breathe and feel the rise and fall of my chest.

I direct attention to the top of my head and move slowly to the bottoms of my feet.

I feel, I bless and give thanks for the body temple.

I am the Watcher.

I breathe deeply. Are there fragrances in the air? Is the air still or moving?

Are the smells subtle or strong or non-existent?

It matters not. I am the Watcher.

Now my senses sleep and I turn inward to my thoughts and feelings.

There is no condemnation in me. I judge not, I label not.

There is stillness, silence, peace.

Nothing disturbs the calm peace of my soul.

I am the Watcher.

The TRUTH IS SPOKEN, but there is more and there will be more meditative, prayerful ideas to guide you as you open yourself to living the mystical life.

PUTTING ON OUR WINGS

SPEAKING THE TRUTH does not bring us into God's presence. It lifts us to the height of our humanness. It is like rising to the edge of a cliff. We are like the bird prepared for its first flight. There is a great nothingness before us, but in watching other birds fly, we know there is an unseen force which lifts and upholds. So we SPEAK THE TRUTH, the highest truth we know, and rest. Perhaps this process should be called Putting On Our Wings.

This is not a matter of conditioning the mind. The simple truth is that we have the mind of the Christ, and it does not need conditioning. The mind is a doorway through which light passes, and therefore it is to be opened. It is the wick of the candle and is an avenue for the expression of Divine Wisdom that is to shine in our individual lives and in the world.

Mary makes an appointment with a spiritual counselor. Mary explains that she has an important employment decision to make, and she wants help in determining her career direction. The counselor who is aware of the simple life shares with Mary that the decision is not the issue. Her true soul's desire is to KNOW GOD. In this instance, Mary is to become aware of the Presence of God as Wisdom. From this consciousness, the right decision will be made through her.

The counselor's focus is not upon the decision; it is upon God and the Wisdom God is being. After relaxing and entering into the Now, Mary is led to the apex of her human consciousness by a guided meditation. A series of affirmations and denials are used, not to condition the mind, but to lift the counselor and Mary to the height of their humanness.

Here is an example of what Mary might have experienced with the counselor.

> *I am the light of the world. And infinite wisdom lives in me.*
> *There is nothing to fear. There is no indecision in me.*
> *I have the mind of the Christ.*
> *I hear the call to let my light shine.*
> *I put aside any choices facing me. Only one thing is needful…*
> *To experience the light that dwells in me, to let it shine.*
> *Each choice is a call for light.*
> *A call to turn to the Source of all Light, to wisdom Itself.*
> *Decisions are put aside. I make only one decision—to turn to the light.*
> *To turn to God knowing light is what I am.*
> *I am the light of the world, and I let it shine.*

The truth is spoken, and then we ask it to be revealed to us. Remember, this is part of a developing relationship with God. It is the same as getting to know anyone. We talk for a while about what we think is true, and then we wait for the other party to reveal his truth. In this case, we rise to the pinnacle of our humanity and wait to be lifted into an awareness of what it is to be made in the image and after the likeness of God. By Putting On Our Wings, our prayer life unfolds, and we are prepared for the next step in the mystical process of daily living – LEARNING TO WAIT.

****

CHAPTER SUMMARY

BY SPEAKING THE TRUTH, I AM LIFTED TO THE HEIGHT OF MY HUMANNESS WHERE, BY GRACE, I AM LIFTED INTO SPIRITUAL CONSCIOUSNESS.

CHAPTER FOUR
LEARNING TO WAIT

GETTING TO KNOW YOU

A mystic knows the art of WAITING and LISTENING. These delicate tools prepare us and make us pliable, so the hand of Spirit can shape our lives. These qualities of the one who lives the mystical life are the chief ingredients of any relationship. In the simple life, the unfolding relationship is with God, and it is similar to times we share with friends. For instance, whenever we are getting to know another person, we tell our friend our inner feelings, concerns, and desires. Then we say, "Now tell me about yourself." As our friend answers with honesty, we grow closer to one another. Listening and waiting for our friend's sharing binds us together, and we discover our oneness. When listening is our first bond, oneness is assured.

There are differences in developing a relationship with a friend and developing conscious oneness with Spirit. There are also consistencies. We "talk" to God, but not to inform the all knowing Presence about ourselves. Remember, we are God's creation. The "talking" (talking may be a thought process) or SPEAKING THE TRUTH, as we referred to it in the previous chapter, reminds us of the truth of our being and the principles governing our lives. SPEAKING THE TRUTH raises us to the apex of our humanity, but we are destined to go higher. Divinity, an experience of the Presence of God, awaits us. It WAITS for us to WAIT.

In the initial stages of WAITING, the mind meanders and wanders in places not conducive to spiritual awakening. We suddenly remember we have forgotten to turn off the oven, or wonder whether we have locked the front door. If we are speaking the truth of wholeness, a "voice" may direct us to ignore the truth and "get realistic." The mind fluttering as a butterfly is normal.

As the mind wanders like the prodigal, it is good to bring it gently home with a simple idea. For instance, if we desire to KNOW GOD as life and wholeness, we might slowly, in rhythm with our breathing,

SPEAK THE TRUTH: I AM WHOLE, AND I AM DIVINE LIFE BEING LIVED. Whenever the mind meanders, we do not resist. We return to this truth. We are not trying to condition the mind or convince ourselves of the validity of the truth we have thought or spoken. We are SPEAKING THE TRUTH and WAITING for Spirit to reveal the essence of the statement I AM WHOLE, AND I AM DIVINE LIFE BEING LIVED. By mentally speaking the truth, we are not free. Jesus said, "...KNOW the truth, and the truth will make you free." John 8:32. Spiritual truth can only be taught by God, and thus revelation is the way of transformation.

And so, like the prophets of old, we WAIT. The promise is "...they who WAIT for the Lord shall renew their strength..." Isaiah 40:31. Our expectation is for no particular happening or phenomenon. We WAIT for the Lord, the Spirit of truth; we WAIT for the coming of the revelation, an experience of the Presence of God.

THE SPOKEN WORD

As the WAITING continues, the time comes when the Word is spoken. This is the experience of the Presence of God. The phrase, THE SPOKEN WORD, refers to the first chapter of Genesis where it is written, "And God said,..." Reading the creation story reveals an obvious truth. Whenever the Word is spoken, a creative power is expressed.

Please realize, no human being SPEAKS THE WORD. We SPEAK THE TRUTH, but only God can SPEAK THE WORD. Remember, we are developing a relationship with our Friend. Is it possible for us to speak for our companion? Who is best qualified to tell the wonders of our Friend's life other than our Friend? Let us learn the art of WAITING. The result of this simple act is that the WORD IS SPOKEN, and a creative power is expressed in our lives and released as a blessing to all humankind.

As we learn the art of WAITING, our lives unfold with wonder and with seeming ease. We WAIT, but not to hear a sound. In fact, the human consciousness hears nothing. It is not attuned to the still, small voice. The SPOKEN WORD is evidence of the Presence of God and is not to be determined or anticipated by us.

This experience of KNOWING GOD is called Silence, for there is no awareness of the outer world. The Silence may last an instant or for many minutes or longer, but no matter how long the Silence, it feeds the soul.

Actually, we will not know of the Silence until we return to a state of consciousness which lies in close proximity to the human condition. However, we are not the same individual who first STOOD STILL. We are true to the call to come up higher, and because of our WAITING, we are transformed. The world is seen differently although the condition my remain the same, and because we are in a different state of consciousness, fresh ideas and insights flow through us. Our actions are different, and our friends say to us, "You have changed."

The following is a meditative practice that will help you understand SPEAKING THE WORD and LEARNING TO WAIT.

It is an autumn day. The Sun is shining and a strong breeze stirs the leaves of a great forest. I am watching to see the first leaf fall from a tree, orange and yellow like so many leaves that will release their grip and follow the one.

I wait and watch. The wind blows like a sigh across the forest as if whispering, "Who will be the first?" I wait and watch. Observant, seeing all. Patient. Quiet. Waiting. Watching.

I see it and can feel its freedom.

Twisting and turning. Letting go. Not knowing where it will come to rest.

Carried by an unseen presence. The Spirit wind, gentle.

I no longer hold on; I am being held.

Like the leaf, I let myself be carried to some unknown place.

Where Spirit wants me to be.

I give no direction to the wind. There is no yearning in me...

Other than to be held.

I let go and let God be God.

And I wait...

Swirling, turning, I come to rest.

In a stream of gently flowing water. Up and down, right and left.

Once more, I let go.

Jim Rosemergy

*Spiritual forces carry me.
As they always have…*

****

CHAPTER SUMMARY

I WAIT FOR GOD TO SPEAK THE WORD. — Yes!

CHAPTER FIVE
LET THERE BE...

THE INNER CLICK

After God SPEAKS THE WORD, and we realize we have experienced the Presence of God, it is appropriate to give thanks. This is an effortless act, for the soul is naturally grateful for the discovery of its spiritual essence. An "inner click" is sensed, and we know we have touched the hem of the garment. Three realizations will be present whenever we are consciously in the Presence. First, we recognize there is only God. Because of this, a second awareness quickly follows: there is nothing to overcome. We have no sense of a foe to defeat or contention of any kind. Finally, because we are in spiritual consciousness, we "see" nothing to fix, alter, or change. This is apparent, for the illusion has passed and the reality of God's creation is evident.

The fruit of WAITING brings us this reward. It is an art appearing passive and without merit, but it is actually faith and trust in disguise. Now we are prepared to learn the art of LETTING. It was good enough for God ("Let there be light; and there was light." Genesis 1:4.), and therefore it is good enough for us.

One of our challenges as human beings is trying too hard. In many cultures, there is a work ethic. This philosophy espouses that if we work hard, we will reach our goals. If this has been our way of life, it is not surprising we apply it to the spiritual path. However, Jesus cautioned us when He spoke of people trying to take the kingdom of God by violence (Matthew 11:12). Obviously, literally we do not attempt such a thing, but in subtle ways we do try to take the kingdom by force—by force of will. To take the kingdom by force is to endeavor to KNOW GOD through an act of will. This is impossible, but it has never stopped us from trying.

In our highest church rhetoric, we place our "deal" before the throne. "O Holy Father, creator of heaven and earth (maybe flattery will help), if you heal me, I will go to church every Sunday." Or perhaps we believe reading the right book will lift us into an awareness of God. We become learned and have the right answers to people's questions, but we don't seem to have solutions for our life's problems. Maybe we attend classes consistently, and workshops and seminars occupy our weekends. However, because there is no waiting or letting, God, the core and "ground of our being," remains elusive.

It is like attempting to enter a beautiful room by smashing down the door. We run against it, throw ourselves upon it, but the door never yields to us. Finally, in a state of exhaustion, we discover the door opens toward us rather than away from us. The need is to step back from the door and allow it to swing open. This is the art of LETTING. No amount of battering opens it.

LET GO THE CONTROLS

Another illustration of letting go occurs when a student pilot learns to fly. In the training program, the student flies a sortie in which he learns how to recover from a potentially disastrous spin. After sufficient altitude is achieved, the instructor pulls up the nose of the aircraft, kicks the rudder, and puts the plane in a spin. Then he says to the student, "It's all yours."

The student thinks, "Who wants it?" A struggle may ensue in which the student grapples with the controls and tries too hard. The spin progressively worsens. Finally, the instructor says, "Let go the controls." After a brief hesitation, the student complies, and the aircraft recovers from the spin. Often our efforts are detrimental, and we need to LET go. If there is to be action, it must come from the guidance emerging from within.

In life we try to recover from spins called illness, a lost job, or a broken relationship. Action seems essential, but LETTING is God's way. Once we experience the inner click alerting us to God's presence, it is time to draw a deep breath and allow God to be God in our lives. The wonder of the spiritual life is upon us, and we are to stay out of its way.

CAN YOU GIVE AN ILLUSTRATION FROM YOUR LIFE WHEN YOU WERE IN A "SPIN" AND TRIED TOO HARD? PLEASE DESCRIBE THE SITUATION IN THE SPACE PROVIDED.

DO YOU RECALL IN STAND STILL, CHAPTER ONE, WHY THE SPIN GETS WORSE RATHER THAN BETTER? (THE ANSWER IS GIVEN AT THE END OF THIS CHAPTER.)

HOW DID YOU EVENTUALLY RECOVER FROM YOUR SPIN? PLEASE WRITE YOUR ANSWER BELOW. *unity principles, affirmations, readings!*

MEEKNESS

One of the beatitudes becomes an important reminder of the art of LETTING and the mystical way of life. "Blessed are the meek for they shall inherit the earth." Matthew 5:5. Meekness does not appear to be the way anyone conquers the earth, however it does not say conquer; it says inherit. An inheritance is something we receive as a result of what we are rather than what we do. It is based on our heritage and in this case, our spiritual roots.

Meekness is our way, meekness toward God. It is allowing Spirit to have Its way with us. This level of trust comes with the understanding that LIFE IS CONSCIOUSNESS. We are no longer trying to direct the course of our lives. We are LETTING an imprisoned splendor escape from within us.

Meekness is non-resistance, for we know that once a state of consciousness is developed, it will naturally manifest itself without additional effort from us. There is meekness in allowing Spirit to do Its work, and there is meekness which comes from the spiritual understanding that our awareness of God is the ultimate womb or center from which life is birthed.

We give thanks that God has SPOKEN THE WORD and LET the consciousness we have experienced unfold in our lives. We may have to act now, or it may be that our guidance is to rest. The consideration of this final step in joining the mystical life and daily living is found in the next chapter entitled, TO ACT OR NOT TO ACT; THAT IS THE QUESTION.

NOTE: REMEMBER THE QUESTION, "DO YOU RECALL IN STAND STILL, CHAPTER ONE, WHY THE SPIN GETS WORSE RATHER THAN BETTER?"

The answer is that we cannot solve a problem from the level of the problem. We must be lifted into another state of consciousness. LETTING allows us to be lifted higher in awareness. Grappling is a function of the attitude which created the problem initially.

****

CHAPTER SUMMARY

AS I EXPERIENCE THE PRESENCE OF GOD, I LET THIS NEWLY ESTABLISHED CONSCIOUSNESS MANIFEST ITSELF IN MY LIFE.

CHAPTER SIX
TO ACT OR NOT TO ACT?
THAT IS THE QUESTION

WILL AND UNDERSTANDING

How natural it is that the mystical life begins with STANDING STILL, and that it eventually carries us into the busy world in which we live, work, and play. From the viewpoint of those who strive to get it done or make it happen, the mystical life seems invalid. Sitting around doing nothing is not going to allow us to contribute to the world or enhance our own life.

However, when we look at the lives of the mystics, we see they were the most active of human beings. They pioneered religious orders, painted works of art, wrote classics that endure through the ages, and were tireless in their service to humanity. In fact, the fruits of their stillness and labor remain to this day. The difference between these seekers of the infinite and the typical person is that the mystic's labor was not an act of will. Willingness was their way, because it is God's way. They learned the fruitlessness of acting without the guidance of Spirit which is the motivating and enlivening factor in any successful endeavor.

In essence, in the lives of those who live the simple life, a union or wedding takes place. In these individuals, will, which acts to accomplish, and understanding, which listens until it knows what to do, are united. When will and understanding are not in accord with one another, the ensuing divorce leads to willfulness and efforts not in service to others. Only self is served and ultimately not served well. When will and understanding are mated, there is willingness and our actions bless us and others.

CAN YOU THINK OF A TIME IN YOUR LIFE WHEN WILL AND UNDERSTANDING WERE NOT UNITED? IT WAS A TIME WHEN YOU ACTED, BUT WITHOUT INNER DIRECTION FROM GOD. PLEASE

INDICATE IN THE SPACE BELOW WHAT YOU DID AND WHAT HAPPENED. *I married my first husband despite some inner instinct that he was rushing me to matrimony. After 4+ years, he abandoned the marriage and our 2 children.*

THE MYSTIC, A BUSY PERSON IN A BUSY WORLD

This is why we initially do nothing. We understand the necessity of being lifted in consciousness before action steps are taken. We comprehend the necessary union of will and understanding. If these two faculties of the soul are not wed, the actions we pursue come from the beliefs that created the problem. So we wait, knowing that the wisdom of God experienced by us may call us to undertake a divine mission. It is also understood that our guidance might be to continue to rest.

For instance, Matthew is a person with many problems, and it is easy to see what the corrections must be. We have tried to help by sharing our experience with him, but to no avail. We ask the Spirit of Truth within us to assist (We will discuss this process in the next section.) and find our guidance is to say and do nothing. Speculation reveals that before we share our understanding of life with another, there must be receptivity. Perhaps at this time, Matthew is not prepared to act. Thus the all-knowing Christ Mind directs our silence and lack of action.

At another time our inner leading is to act. In fact, what we are called to do may seem beyond us, or it calls for such a change in our lives that it seems impossible. Being guided to apply for ministerial school is a good example. Upon acceptance we may begin to doubt our commitment and capabilities. Or as we attend classes and work full time, the demand may seem beyond our energy and strength.

A person can be guided to begin a business and therefore looks at the resources required to accomplish such a task. During these moments, it is good to remember that divine direction comes complete. If money is required, it is available. If people are necessary, they are moving into the sphere of our lives, and if we continue to be tuned in, we will recognize them.

CHECKING IN EACH DAY

Checking in each day is a good practice to remember. We may be guided to initiate a project, but we must not just say thank you to Spirit and then forsake daily direction. The mystical approach to living requires a daily commitment. We must check in consistently.

A couple once felt genuinely guided to start a business in which they provided gravel and sand to construction companies. A geological deposit was purchased and financing arranged, so equipment could be bought. Many decisions were made, but one was their downfall. The road built to the site was inadequate. When the large dump trucks first came, all went well and as expected, the business thrived. Later the rainy season began, and the road could not bear the weight of the trucks and the tonnage they carried. The trucks became stuck, and the new owners paid for wreckers to pull the trucks from the mud. Soon the road was worthless, loans came due, but there was no cash flow to pay the monthly bills. The business collapsed. If the owners had "checked in" with Spirit, they probably would have been guided to build a better road.

The mystical life is not sitting beneath trees. It only begins with sitting. Then it lifts us into the realm of Spirit and provides God with an able servant. Our lives are blessed, and we become God in action. Service is rendered blessing humankind. Silence is "broken" by God SPEAKING THE WORD. STANDING STILL is put aside as we act boldly and swiftly under the tutorage of Spirit. The tutorage of Spirit which is the key to the question, to act or not to act.

While we are in human consciousness, we act blindly and in response to our will. It is best that we do nothing, for what we do does us and others a disservice. Once we are lifted into an awareness of God, there is willingness, and what we do serves all humankind. So let us act, but only when the movement of our hands and feet and the expression of our thoughts are imbued with the love, peace, and wisdom of our God.

CAN YOU GIVE AN EXAMPLE FROM YOUR LIFE WHEN YOU WERE ATTUNED TO SPIRIT? THE INNER DIRECTION YOU FELT AND RESPONDED TO MAY NOT HAVE MADE SENSE AT THE TIME, BUT AFTER

Jim Rosemergy

AWHILE THE WISDOM OF THE ACTION WAS CLEAR. PLEASE TELL OF YOUR ACTION IN THE SPACE PROVIDED BELOW.

I made several improvements to my home on Oneida St to get it ready for sale and we receive above the price we had listed it for. I wanted to move to VA Bch and we did.

****

CHAPTER SUMMARY

FROM THE CENTER THAT IS GOD, I NOW ACT AND EVEN THE SIMPLEST TASK IS SACRED, FOR IT IS GOD'S WORK.

CONCLUSION AND SUMMARY OF THE MYSTICAL PATH

The six steps of the mystical life are based on the experience of those who live without illusion and for whom the simplest act is sacred, for its center is an awareness of God. This is not a life for a few, but the destiny of the many. It begins by STANDING STILL and culminates with God-directed action or inaction. The steps joining stillness and action are principles shunned by our humanity, but embraced by our divinity.

The second step is BEING STILL. In brief, it is the acknowledgment that God is the answer. Only a consciousness of God yields the life we seek. The goals and ambitions of our human selves are set aside, and the soul mounts up in its single desire to KNOW GOD.

Next, we SPEAK THE TRUTH, the highest truth we know. We are taken to the height of our human consciousness, but a little lower than the angels. By LEARNING TO WAIT, the fourth step in the mystical process, we are lifted into a consciousness of Spirit. The Word is spoken by God, and spiritual power is released and expressed.

Naturally, we give thanks and enter the fifth step, LETTING. The new consciousness we are lifted into is now manifesting itself. It is best we allow it to bless us and not abort the simple life by trying to direct the course of our lives. If there is to be ACTION, the final step in the mystical process, it will become evident, and then boldly and peacefully we will serve our God.

SECTION TWO

INTRODUCTION

The mystical teachings, once cloistered for thousands of years, are now placed in every human hand. For too long, these spiritual ideals were practiced by only a few individuals. One reason is that religion's creed promised peace and joy after death while avoiding the cry of the masses for help with the current issues of illness, poverty, and war. Naturally, the response of the people involved with these trials was a creed declaring religion impractical and without merit. Perhaps the reason for a lack of faith in religion is that religion lacked faith in the ability of every person to directly experience the Presence of God.

Today two challenges are issued. God's gauntlet is for humankind to apply the principles of the simple life to every situation experienced in daily living. Our dare is the same one placed before every religion and every spiritual teacher. Can your ideals help me live my life? Will the principles enable me to make wise decisions or heal my ailing wife? Can your way of life fulfill its promise of loving relationships? Can you help me provide for my family?

The true answer to these questions is not given by clergy. The principles of the mystical life are not to be substantiated by the rhetoric and debates of religious scholars, but by men and women facing the challenges of everyday living. Willingness to commit to the steps of the simple life is paramount, but it is even more important that this path lead to a closer relationship with God and to peace and joy which do not depend upon what happens in the world.

Words may inspire and ideas may bring hope, but only experience is the supreme teacher. It requires courage to live the simple life, as well as the inner conviction that Being holds meaning and value beyond what appears important. The time has come to pick up the gauntlet God has placed before us and to test the practicality of the mystical life.

In LIVING THE MYSTICAL LIFE TODAY, the problems of earthly existence are categorized in four major areas: decision-making, human relationships, prosperity, and health and wholeness. In Section

Two, each of these areas of concern serves as an example of how to apply the steps of the simple life.

Please do not view this section and its examples as solely material to read, but as a handbook for practical, dynamic living. Each category of human concern is approached from the mystical perspective, and as the reader adopts the same viewpoint, problems are solved, but more importantly, a deeper awareness of God is experienced. Read the ideas relevant to the problem area in your life, and then let prayer and meditation prepare you to experience the Presence of God, for this is the heart of the mystical life. Reading and meditating are only the beginning of this spiritual odyssey, for what awaits you is the simple life.

CHAPTER SEVEN
DECISION MAKING

THE PROBLEM

Stan is a minister who pioneered a church that is now expressing the power and wisdom of God in the community. There is contentment and joy as well as commitment on the part of many people to continue to grow spiritually. The people are excited and many sense the rising power of Spirit as possibilities of rendering greater service to individuals seeking a closer walk with God.

Then suddenly, there is the possibility Stan will leave to serve another ministry. Reason denies the potential move, but Stan has always remained open to the guidance of Spirit. Therefore, the likelihood of assuming the leadership of another church causes him to apply the steps of the simple life to his situation.

On the surface, a decision must be made. However, the first step of the simple life is to STAND STILL. Life seems filled with many decisions: where will we live, what career should we pursue, when do we leave the relationship? Inner revelation reveals THERE IS ONLY ONE DECISION TO MAKE. Either we turn within to the Spirit of Truth for direction, or we turn to the many confusing voices of the world.

For Stan, the issue is not whether he should leave one ministry to serve another. BEING STILL reminds him that his purpose is to know and experience the Presence of God as Wisdom.

The question of what ministry to serve is put aside. Stan's attention is given to God, for a discovery is to be made. Stan is to realize he has the mind of Christ. The light of divine wisdom is to shine. He exhibits no preference as to where he will live. His strong desire is to KNOW GOD as Light. Once this consciousness is experienced, decisions are not made; they shine as right choices. Remember, God's way is LET your light shine.

As Stan's purpose is clarified, he takes the third step of the simple life. He SPEAKS THE TRUTH. The statements of truth he speaks or thinks lift him out of confusion and indecision to the periphery of his human consciousness. However, there is nothing a human being can do to raise himself into the kingdom of God. No amount of human striving can bring us to God. Spirit must ultimately come to us and bring us to Itself. Our work is to turn homeward like the prodigal son by SPEAKING THE TRUTH and WAITING. Then Spirit "comes" to us while we are still far from home (still in human consciousness).

Each day Stan sits, SPEAKS THE TRUTH, and WAITS. He does not want to know what to do, but instead desires to KNOW GOD as Wisdom. Undoubtedly, light (a decision) will "shine" from this awareness of God. During these times of stillness and quietude, a gift is given to Stan. The phrase, let there be light, emerges in his mind and comforts him. Thanksgiving is expressed and when needed, the decision comes. Action is taken, and Stan departs for the new ministry. More than a decision emerged. A consciousness of divine wisdom was established through which light may always shine.

The following series of meditative statements are examples of truth Stan may have spoken as he sought to experience the Presence of God as wisdom and light.

> *I stand still.*
> *My yearning is not to know what to do.*
> *It is to experience my God.*
> *I have only one choice.*
> > *I either turn within to God*
> > *Or I turn without to the world.*
> *I know what to do.*
> > *I speak the highest truth I know*
> > *And I wait…*
> *I have the mind of the Christ.*
> *It is the wisdom God is that I seek.*
> *I seek no guidance; I seek an awareness that God is wisdom.*
> *I hear the ancient call, "You are the light of the world; let your light shine."*
> *God is light and that light is shining.*
> *It radiates in and through and as me.*

I wait...
There is no doubt or concern in me.
No fear of tomorrow.
I let the light shine.
And I wait...

In Stan's case, he had ample time to sit and move through the steps of the mystical life. Obviously, this is not always possible, for situations often demand immediate and decisive action. This is why the simple life is food for daily living. As we sit and turn our attention Godward each day, a reservoir of consciousness is built up on which we can always rely. This is why Jesus and every follower of the mystical path rest in silence daily.

A RESERVOIR OF CONSCIOUSNESS

Consider a checkbook. We may not write checks and make purchases each day, but if there are funds in the account, they can be relied upon. If there is no money in the account, even though we may want to buy something, this is not possible. Spiritually, our account is a reservoir of consciousness built up by DAILY deposits or times of prayer and meditation. Then whenever an immediate decision is to be made (like which way do we turn to avoid the child who has rushed into the street from between two parked cars), the light shines without effort or thought. Therefore, the mystical approach to living requires daily attention.

GROUP DECISIONS

The principles associated with individual decision making also apply to corporate or group decisions. This is desirable, for the divine light is to shine in all human endeavors. In this way, God's Spirit is expressed in all things. Perhaps it is true to say that the choices we are to make are actually opportunities for the light to shine.

When a group desires to listen to and heed the Spirit of Truth, it follows the same process as the individual. After the time of meditation, prayer, or quiet, each person shares his or her experience and feeling as to what should be done. Often what was once an agonizing decision is now readily apparent. At other times, there is no clear direction revealed to the group, so no action is taken, and the process is repeated at another time.

****

CHAPTER SUMMARY

DECISIONS ARE MADE AS I EXPERIENCE THE WISDOM OF GOD AND LET IT SHINE THROUGH ME.

PRINCIPLES OF THE SIMPLE LIFE FOR DECISION MAKING

1. THERE IS ONLY ONE DECISION TO MAKE, EITHER I TURN WITHIN TO GOD OR WITHOUT TO THE WORLD.
2. ONCE I TURN WITHIN, THE CHOICE I AM TO MAKE IS NO LONGER THE ISSUE.
3. NO PREFERENCE IS MADE AS TO WHAT I WOULD LIKE TO DO OR HAVE HAPPEN.
4. MY PURPOSE IS TO KNOW AND EXPERIENCE GOD AS LIGHT AND WISDOM.
5. I FOLLOW THE SIX STEPS OF THE SIMPLE LIFE.
6. THE ACTION STEP TO BE TAKEN IS MADE KNOWN TO ME WHEN IT IS NEEDED, NOT BEFORE.

CHAPTER EIGHT
HUMAN RELATIONSHIPS

THE PROBLEM

Lori is involved with George, a married man. He tells her his marriage is in name only and that he and his wife have an "understanding." Once the youngest child who is sixteen enrolls in college, George will be able to divorce his wife and marry Lori. This is not the first time Lori has been in a relationship with a married man. This time she hopes "things" will work out, and that she and George will be married.

For five months Lori and George seem suited for one another, but then the breakup begins. George no longer calls as often as he once did, and during the times they are together, few words are spoken. The sensitivity which once marked the relationship disappears, and finally George informs Lori that he will not be calling her again.

Feelings of hurt, rejection, and abandonment overwhelm Lori. She has felt them before, but they are now so intense she is unable to work. She contacts a spiritually oriented counselor who shares with her a new approach to her problem. Lori's willingness to try something different is her new beginning, and eventually she breaks the pattern which has plagued her life for many years.

During Lori's counseling sessions, she and her counselor discussed her feelings and the unhealthy pattern of her relationships with men. Then the adviser began to explain the principles of the simple life as they apply to loving human relationships. First, Lori was told that the issue is not George, or her involvement with men. The answer lies in her relationship with God.

LAWS OF LOVE

We often believe we lack love and that it can be acquired from other people. Therefore, a great effort is expended to appear attractive and to get others to love us. We enter into relationships from a consciousness of lack (we believe we lack love), and naturally we do not find the love we think we lack.

The truth is, God is love and we are made in the image and after the likeness of God. Simple logic declares our nature is love. We lack nothing but an awareness of our divine essence. The simple life directs us, not to search for love in the arms and soft words of another, but in the realization that unless there is love without people, there is never love with them.

In the mystical way of life, the focus is not upon releasing hurt feelings or forgiving the perpetrator of our anguish. The rejection we experience is the result of a state of consciousness in which we believe we lack love. The need is not to become a more pleasing person who is worthy of someone's love, or to be free of negative emotions. When we are STILL, we know our purpose is to KNOW GOD as Love. As we rise into this state of awareness, we leave behind unforgiving thoughts and vengeance and enter into the kingdom of God where love is king.

In fact, for a period of time it is best that we avoid relationships. It is time to get to know ourselves and to discover we are love. Therefore, the TRUTH IS SPOKEN and we WAIT. We ascend to the apex of our humanity and pause so God can take us higher.

The following is an example of the prayer and meditative process Lori may have used to support her willingness to experience God as Love.

> *I no longer turn to the world or men for love.*
> *Love is closer than hands and feet and breathing.*
> *Love is more than a part of me.*
> *Love is the essence of my being.*
> *God is Love and I am made in Love's image.*
> *Love is closer than I think.*
> *I place my hand over my heart...*
> *And feel the beating of divine love in my being.*
> *I am here; God is here, and all is well.*
> *I am completely filled with love.*
> *I am a cup overflowing.*

> *I feel my unity with all life.*
> *It is a part of me, I am a part of it.*
> *Unified with creation, I am not alone.*
> *There is only One, and I am an expression of that One.*
> *The One that is Love...*
> *I wait...*
> > *Love is what I am*
> > *Seeking ceases.*
> > *I am all I seek, all I need.*
> > *I am love.*
> *I wait...trusting, listening...*
> *Patiently, I wait.*

Day by day Lori entered into this process until the breakthrough occurred. She felt love, and no one was present. Lori discovered the Presence of God and her divine nature. Now, the love expressed by Lori is not an attempt to receive love from another so her void is filled, but an expression of who and what she is. This love is unconditional, for its expression is its own fulfillment.

Lori's past actions denied she was made in the image and after the likeness of Love. Now anything she says and does from a consciousness of divine love will affirm her true nature. Undoubtedly, her relationships with men will be different. She no longer needs love, for she has found love is what she is.

In the future if Lori experiences hurt or rejection, she will know she is to STAND STILL and remember her purpose is to KNOW GOD as Love. She will SPEAK THE TRUTH and then WAIT until the remembrance of who she is reestablishes itself in her soul. From this center, she will act in ways that are loving and kind.

****

CHAPTER SUMMARY

MY HUMAN RELATIONSHIPS ARE HARMONIZED AS I DISCOVER I AM LOVE.

PRINCIPLES OF THE SIMPLE LIFE FOR HARMONIOUS HUMAN RELATIONSHIPS

1. HUMAN RELATIONSHIPS ARE NOT THE ISSUE.
2. GOD IS LOVE, AND BECAUSE I AM MADE IN THE IMAGE AND AFTER THE LIKENESS OF GOD, I DO NOT LACK LOVE.
3. LOVE IS MY NATURE.
4. UNLESS THERE IS LOVE WITHOUT PEOPLE, THERE IS NO LOVE WITH THEM.
5. KNOWING AND EXPERIENCING GOD AS LOVE IS MY ASPIRATION.
6. I FOLLOW THE STEPS OF THE SIMPLE LIFE.

CHAPTER NINE
PROSPERITY

THE PROBLEM

Wayne and his wife, Julie, have a two-year-old son. The family has struggled financially for the past three years. Julie has not worked since Josh's birth, and Wayne is steadily employed only during the summer. Both Wayne and Julie know there is a need for change in their lives. They learn of a prosperity course entitled, "The Mystical Search for Riches," which is being taught at a neighborhood church, and they decide to attend. The idea of spiritual principles and laws governing financial freedom is strange to them, but their situation demands a new approach.

While attending the class, Wayne and Julie are exposed to the simple life. They learn to STAND STILL, and to realize that money to meet financial obligations is not the real issue in their lives. Repeatedly, the teacher reminds the class of the mystical search and inner security. Understandably, tangible needs seem all consuming, but the purpose of the study is to become aware that God is the Source. At first, Wayne and Julie are offended when they are asked to cease focusing on the immediate needs in their lives, but they are also fascinated by the breakthroughs occurring in the lives of some of their classmates. They hope similar employment opportunities come to them.

THE PRINCIPLES

The teacher stresses the idea of "seek first his kingdom…and all these things shall be yours as well." Matthew 6:33. The young couple is shocked to learn that the kingdom is not a far away place where God dwells, but an awareness of God to be experienced by each person. This consciousness of Spirit is the Source and Provider. Wayne and Julie's focus is shifting, for by BEING STILL they are true to Jesus' statement, "Therefore take no thought, saying What shall we eat, or What shall we drink?…" Matthew 6:31 KJV. No longer are they obsessed with their earthly needs. The desire to KNOW GOD is their purpose.

UNDERSTANDING THE PAST

When their attention was upon what they did not have, their consciousness became a seed yielding worse conditions. Initially, it was difficult to pay the rent each month, and soon the electric company threatened to terminate services. For three years, the family experienced Jesus' statement: "For to everyone who has will more be given, and he will have abundance (those who think abundantly, experience greater and greater abundance); but from him who has not, even what he has will be taken away." Matthew 25:29. "Him who has not" is the person obsessed by what he lacks. Even what he has is taken away because thoughts of lack produce after their kind.

The understanding of this principle enables Wayne and Julie to understand the past three years of deprivation and frustration. They are also aware that they must live the principles of the simple life if they are to become those who will have abundance.

However, the abundance addressed in class is not of this world. The instructor stresses the mystical process of rising into an awareness of God. The TRUTH IS SPOKEN and together the class WAITS and anticipates the Presence of God. In this prayerful state, there is no asking and not even the assurance of tangible needs being fulfilled. Remember, the simple life is not of this world, so we take no thought about what we shall eat, drink, or wear. Instead, we yearn for God, and our need is fulfilled. There is contentment and the realization that the fields are "white unto harvest." We join Paul in hearing the voice of the Christ, "My grace is sufficient for you..." II Corinthians 12:9.

MOVE YOUR FEET

From this consciousness of God, we act (move our feet) in ways declaring Spirit is our Provider. There is no longer fear in giving. Making ends meet becomes a circle of giving and receiving. In the past, we did not give, for we viewed giving as a producer of lack. We did not see it as an affirmation that God is our Source. We failed to comprehend that when the hand is extended to give, it is also prepared to receive. We receive, not according to God's capacity to give, but according to our capacity to receive.

In fact, the dynamic of receiving is seen differently from the mystical vantage point than from the human perspective. Receiving, like asking, is no longer of the world. To receive is to awaken to God's presence. It is to eat at the table God prepares, for did Jesus not say, "I have food to eat of which you do not know"? John 4:32. Surely, He ate at this table in His times of prayer. The food or nourishment received is the food we have not known; it is a consciousness of Spirit, our all sufficiency.

THE SIMPLE METHOD

Wayne and Julie are participating fully in the prosperity class. They do not understand all they hear, but they are eager and willing students. Much of the class is spent in stillness as the teacher leads the students in meditations focused upon God. The class contemplates the feeding of the five thousand. They join the Hebrews in puzzling and rejoicing over the manna. Their thoughts turn to the ravens which fed the prophet, and peace and security are more deeply experienced.

Each time Wayne and Julie are still, they feel better, and changes are taking place in their lives. Added things are the result of their inner work. A year round job opportunity comes to Wayne, and Julie discovers that her sewing skills increase the family income. They are giving and feeling the joy of contributing to God's work in the world.

They are delightfully startled when the teacher tells the class that humankind's nature is to give. Tithing is explained during the evening, not as giving ten percent of their income to a church, but as a declaration that God is first in their lives. By giving (ten percent seems a just amount) to their channel of spiritual good, the truth of being is affirmed, and God's message of truth is carried into the world.

Wayne and Julie's faith is growing. They are becoming more aware of their Source, and out of the stillness, ideas and actions are coming. They may not know the channel of their good tomorrow, but they understand their consciousness of God provides a daily bread. The manna is appreciated and observed as a part of their lives. They are secure, for they follow the mystical path.

The following prayerful and meditative statements can be used by anyone to help him/her become aware that God is the Source.

I stand still and start with what I have.
And what I have I bless, I give thanks.
Thanksgiving opens me.
    The scales fall from my eyes.
    The fields are white unto harvest...even in the winter.
    The trees bear fruit in every season, for God is my Source.
I am the place where the divine supply appears.
    I am sensitive to ideas, to opportunities.
    God is moving in my life.
    First in unseen ways, but I am waiting and watching.
I give thanks and I give of the blessings of my life.
    I enter the circle that never ends, to refresh and renew.
    And as I give, I am aware of manna on the ground.
    Of ideas emerging, of feelings of security flooding my being.
The Lord is my Shepherd. I do not want.
    I cannot want.
    God is my source.
    Asking ceases.
I am prospered. I have God. I have all I need.
I wait...content, peaceful, safe and secure.
I wait...

                ****

CHAPTER SUMMARY

I AM PROSPERED BY GOD'S PRESENCE AND BLESSED TO BE A BLESSING.

PRINCIPLES OF THE SIMPLE LIFE FOR PROSPERITY

1. SEEK FIRST THE KINGDOM...AND ALL THESE THINGS SHALL BE YOURS AS WELL.

2. I TAKE NO THOUGHT OF WHAT I AM TO EAT, DRINK, OR WEAR.
3. MONEY, EMPLOYMENT, AND "MAKING ENDS MEET" ARE NOT THE ISSUE.
4. MY PURPOSE IS TO REALIZE GOD'S PRESENCE IS MY PROSPERITY.
5. I FOLLOW THE STEPS OF THE SIMPLE LIFE.
6. IT IS MY NATURE TO GIVE.
7. MY CONSCIOUSNESS OF GOD PROVIDES MY DAILY BREAD.

CHAPTER TEN
HEALING

THE PROBLEM

Jonathan is diagnosed as terminally ill. Seemingly, he is in perfect health, but suddenly a week ago, while jogging, he experienced a sharp pain in his lower abdomen. He thought the problem would go away, but as the evening continued the discomfort intensified. He called a friend who took him to the hospital. X-rays indicated a mass in Jonathan's intestines, so he was admitted to the hospital for further tests. The doctor's worst prognosis was confirmed, for Jonathan has an inoperable cancerous tumor.

There is little the physicians can do for Jonathan, however he knows there is another approach to his problem. For the past year, he had committed himself to the simple life, and therefore understands that with God nothing is impossible. He is aware he is made in the image and after the likeness of God. Because of this truth, he knows wholeness is his destiny. In the past, Jonathan would have bargained with God. "God, if you give me my health, I'll go to the church of Your choice each Sunday. I'll..."

Jonathan is now aware of a spiritual principle expressed by a 20th century mystic, Joel Goldsmith. WHAT GOD CAN DO, GOD IS DOING. There is no need to ask God to heal him. God is being life, and in this divine life there is no disease.

The first step in the process of healing is not a desire for the restoration of the body, but a desire to awaken to an awareness of divine life. As we have seen before, the problem, in this case a healing need, is not the issue. Always, the answer is a consciousness of God.

When we know our spiritual essence is God Life, there is nothing to heal. God is not in the repair business. Spirit does no maintenance. Therefore, it is for us to rise to the height of spiritual perfection where we are whole and lack nothing. This ascent transcends the body and its maladies or even health, but it does not deny the pain and suffering of the human condition. Instead, we understand that in human consciousness there is disease, while in spiritual consciousness there is none. The mystical way is clear. Why live in the valley of human awareness where pain and illness are prevalent when we are destined to live in the height that is the kingdom of God where all people are whole?

THE BODY'S ROLE IN HEALING

Wholeness is not a function of the body. We are not more spiritually whole when we are an athlete performing feats of endurance than when we are in the hospital near death. A finely tuned body does not indicate wholeness anymore than a body exhibiting symptoms hiding wholeness. We are instructed not to judge by appearances.

Wholeness is always present regardless of the condition of the body. Spiritual completeness is constantly waiting for eyes to see and for a consciousness to know. This state of mind is the attending physician, and when this "doctor sees" God's image and likeness AS the patient, all is well. The sign of wellness is not seen in the X-ray, but in the realization that there is nothing to heal. This Godly vision can be seen no matter the condition of the body. We are Spirit, for we are made in the image and after the likeness of divine life.

TO VISUALIZE OR NOT TO VISUALIZE WHOLENESS?

Often we attempt to visualize wholeness by seeing the body functioning perfectly and fulfilling its assigned tasks. For instance, we might envision a person running after a leg is broken, or strong, white blood cells combating weak, disorganized cancer cells. These techniques are helpful and are a step along humankind's spiritual path, but it is now time to step into the kingdom of God where there is nothing to repair and to cease in our efforts to perform maintenance on the human condition.

Moses experienced God's presence and was "told" man is not to make graven images of God, for Spirit is without form and beyond our imaginings. Let us realize a thought is just as much a graven image as a stone statue. We cannot imagine spiritual wholeness. Wholeness defined is the sign that wholeness is still unknown to us. Only in the

Silence do we know our spiritual wholeness, and it is so vast words and images only hint at its fullness.

Wholeness is not a matter of the body; therefore we must ultimately not image the body in perfect working order. Remember, in the mystical life the solving of the problem is not the issue. KNOWING GOD is our purpose. From this experience, things (like healings) are added unto us.

JONATHAN'S METHOD

Jonathan understands these principles and knows this challenge is a call to live the simple life. He has studied it, and now it is time to experience it. After the initial shock, he STANDS STILL and acknowledges that the healing of his body is not his purpose. He is to BE STILL, and KNOW GOD.

He SPEAKS THE TRUTH. Ideas such as these move through his mind when his first thought is God:

God is Life.
I am made in the image and likeness of Life Itself.
What God is, I am.
I am divine life appearing in the world.
I am not the body.
   I am life in expression.
   I am divine life being lived.
   In this life, there is no disease, discomfort or pain.
God fills my whole being.
I am whole, lacking nothing.
I resist not.
All I seek, I am.
All there is is God.
I wait...
   I am under the care of the Great Physician.
I fear not. I stand still.
I seek to know the One.
   This is enough. It reveals the truth of my being.
I am as God created me.

> *Nothing of the world can change what God has made.*
> *I wait...and all is well.*

He rests with these ideas and seeks God, not a healing. He longs for the realization, THERE IS NOTHING TO HEAL. He WAITS for the WORD TO BE SPOKEN. And it is. Jonathan LETS God be God, and action follows. He is guided to begin a regimen of certain foods. He does not eat this diet so he can be healed, but because he is guided to eat it. In the mind of this follower of the simple life, there is nothing to heal. Jonathan takes no thought concerning his body. His mind is stayed on God, and the cancerous mass dissolves.

More than a body is restored. In fact, the added thing, the healing, is the result of Jonathan's commitment to a closer walk with God. Jonathan's consciousness of wholeness is enhanced. For him, wholeness is not of the body, it is of Spirit. This awareness will enable him to help others in their yearning to walk with God.

****

CHAPTER SUMMARY

IN THE SIMPLE LIFE THE ADDED THING CALLED HEALING IS EXPERIENCED WHEN I KNOW WHO I AM.

Who Am I?

Who I am
   cannot be told.
   The telling is in what I'm not.
Who I am
   does not eat the seed of the earth or the fruit of the trees. I drink no water.
Who I am
   doesn't shiver when it's cold and grow weary when it's hot.
   I wear no clothes.
Who I am

Is not pierced by doctor's tools or healed by man's elixir. I am not sick.
Who I am
   lacks nothing.
   And asks nothing of God,
   for what God can do, God is doing.
Who am I?
   I cannot tell.
   Only God can answer.
And when I ask, "Who am I?"
God answers, "Who's asking?"

PRINCIPLES OF THE SIMPLE LIFE FOR HEALING

1. I ASK NOTHING OF GOD. THE HEALING OF MY BODY IS NOT THE ISSUE.
2. I REALIZE WHAT GOD CAN DO, GOD IS DOING. (Joel Goldsmith)
3. GOD IS BEING LIFE.
4. I SEEK NOT A HEALING, BUT A CONSCIOUSNESS OF THE DIVINE LIFE I AM.
5. I LIVE THE STEPS OF THE SIMPLE LIFE.

CHAPTER ELEVEN
HOW TO HELP ANOTHER

HELPLESS NO MORE

Each of us, at some point in our lives, has someone close to us who is experiencing a great challenge. It may be a relative who is ill or a friend who is forlorn because of a lost love. It could be our teenage daughter addicted to drugs and unable or unwilling to stop the senseless destruction of her life. The possibilities are infinite, but the process of rendering assistance from the mystical viewpoint is always the same.

The simple life is especially helpful in helping others. This method's purpose is not to repair the person's life, but to elevate the helper's sight. This restored vision gives the Creator eyes through which to see Its creation.

GOD'S WAY

When we persist in human consciousness, we sometimes attempt to get the other person to see it our way. We share our "wisdom" and wonder why it is not received or appreciated. Actually, some of our attempts to help become a wedge driving us farther apart. We try to manipulate the friend or family member. These and other methods fail for numerous reasons. First, our actions do not rise from an awareness of God. We have ignored the first step of the simple life, STAND STILL. Our actions and advice come from a consciousness of concern, worry, or fear. Is it a surprise our wisdom is not helpful?

Secondly, we try to fix the other person. No one likes a relationship with someone who sees him less than whole. Probably, the person sees himself this way, and therefore he resists someone else seeing him as incomplete. The person with the problem is looking for someone to see him whole. This is the key ingredient of the helping consciousness.

The person in need is God's creation. Conditions and behavior do not change what God has made. We must allow ourselves to be lifted in consciousness until we see nothing to fix and nothing to change or alter. From the human perspective, this is foolishness, but for those who live the mystical life today, it is God's way.

THE HEM OF THE GARMENT

In Jesus' ministry, the mystical method of rendering help is illustrated for us today. A story recorded in three of the gospels (Matthew 9:18–26; Mark 5:21–43; Luke 8:40–56) reveals the principles of how to help another. Jesus is walking to a household where a young girl recently died. He is going to raise the child from the dead. Apparently, there are many people walking with Him, pressing in upon Him. Suddenly, He stops and asks, "Who was it that touched me?" Luke 8:45. The disciples are puzzled by the question, for many people have touched Him, but they fail to realize Jesus' question is an inquiry as to who touched His consciousness, not His clothes.

A woman who has had a flow of blood for twelve years is the one Jesus seeks. As she moved through the throng toward Him, she thought, "If I touch even His garments, I shall be made well." Mark 5:28. She manages to brush His clothing, but her receptivity enabled her to touch the awareness of life and wholeness Jesus was experiencing as He journeyed to raise the little girl from the dead.

Notice in the story that Jesus does not attempt to fix the woman. He is simply centered in God. This is always the work of the healer. We are not to try to heal or change other people, but to KNOW GOD. Through receptivity, the other person touches the hem of this garment or consciousness of the Presence. Please realize the healer is not aware of the person who is sick; the healer is aware of God!

RECEPTIVITY'S ROLE

This is the mystical approach to helping others. God does no maintenance, and neither do we. We are lifted into the kingdom of God where there is no sickness. With this method, it is not necessary for the person in need to understand the principles of the simple life. Receptivity is the work of the person in pain. The woman who touched the hem of Jesus' garment did not understand the principles of healing.

Intellectual understanding is not a prerequisite for healing, for intellectual understanding heals nothing. Only a consciousness of God does this sacred work.

As we become attuned to this process, we understand the great need to come apart awhile each day to maintain and nurture our conscious contact with God. We do not know when a willing soul will call, write, or in some way "reach" and touch our current state of mind. If we are one with God, we are instruments of peace and servants of God. If we are in human consciousness, no assistance is rendered.

PRAYING WITH OR FOR OTHERS?

We do not pray with or for other people. Remember, in the simple life we do not attempt to change individuals. Nor do we ask God to act, for WHAT GOD CAN DO, GOD IS DOING. Instead, we maintain our conscious contact with God and rest as a hem extended to any receptive soul.

As we SPEAK THE TRUTH, it is important we do not give mental suggestions to other people. Therefore, we avoid YOU statements. (YOU ARE WHOLE AND WELL. YOU ARE PEACEFUL AND ATTUNED TO GOD.) Since we are treating ourselves rather than another person, we use I statements. (I AM WHOLE AND WELL. I AM PEACEFUL AND ATTUNED TO GOD.) The TRUTH IS SPOKEN to lift us to the apex of our humanity where we WAIT for God to SPEAK THE WORD. Suddenly, through grace, we are lifted into the kingdom of God or spiritual consciousness. When this occurs, the WORD IS SPOKEN and God's work is evident. This is enough, for when anyone, through receptivity, touches this garment, it is "on earth as it is in heaven." The human condition changes or our view of it is transformed. This is not for us to predict, for often the changes which occur are beyond the confines of the human mind.

The following meditation statements illustrate how to open ourselves to be threads in the hem of the garment.

I am relaxing, drawing a deep breath while knowing that the air I breathe does not sustain me.
I am pure Spirit.

> *I breathe no air, I drink no water, I eat no food.*
> I am pure Spirit.
> > *The Life God Is is the truth of my being.*
> > *Divine Life fills me completely.*
> > *There is no room for anything but God.*
> *I am whole, perfect and complete.*
> > *I am as God created me.*
> > *Nothing of the world changes the truth of my being.*
> *Spirit expresses Itself as me.*
> *All that is needed is provided.*
> *It is a part of what I am.*
> > *There is peace, for peace is what I am.*
> > *There is strength, for strength is what I am.*
> > *There is love, for love is what I am.*
> *There is no lack in me, for I am the fountain where Divine Substance is made manifest.*
> *All is well, for I am born of Spirit.*
> *I am as God created me.*

****

CHAPTER SUMMARY

IN THE SIMPLE LIFE, I RENDER HELP TO OTHERS NOT BY CHANGING THEM, BUT BY RESTING CONSCIOUSLY IN THE PRESENCE OF GOD.

PRINCIPLES OF THE SIMPLE LIFE FOR HELPING OTHERS

1. I REALIZE MY PURPOSE IS NOT TO REPAIR A PERSON'S LIFE, BUT TO SEE WITH THE EYES OF SPIRIT.
2. IN THE KINGDOM OF GOD, THERE IS NOTHING TO CHANGE, ALTER, OR FIX.
3. I FOLLOW THE STEPS OF THE SIMPLE LIFE.
4. I USE "I" STATEMENTS WHEN SPEAKING THE TRUTH, FOR I AM TREATING MYSELF.

5. I MAINTAIN A CONSCIOUS CONTACT WITH GOD IN ORDER TO PERPETUALLY EXTEND THE "GARMENT" TO THOSE IN NEED.

CHAPTER TWELVE
THE SIGN OF THE NEW AGE

A PERSONAL NOTE

The New Age is upon us. We are not far along this path, but we have begun the journey. The signs of the New Age are not seen with the human eye, and its development cannot be pointed to with the human hand, for the New Age's chief signs are STILLNESS and SILENCE. Many feel a New Age person is recognized by words of oneness, a concern for the Earth Mother, or by a strong commitment to world peace. This man or woman may be involved in these areas, but concern for the world is not the focus of the emerging beings of this planet. Remember, in the simple life we are in the world, but not of it. We do not seek to change or repair the world. The quest is to rise into God's Presence where there is nothing to mend.

As the New Age is established and the mystical path begins to become the accepted approach to daily living, STILLNESS and SILENCE will be cherished. Corporations and small businesses as well as schools shall encourage times of reflection for employees, teachers, and students. Inaction rather than action will be valued, for many will understand that enduring accomplishments originate in the seemingly passive quiet of the soul. People in all walks of life will seek an awareness of God. It shall be understood that "nothing is so like God as STILLNESS." (Meister Eckhart) SILENCE will not be the absence of sound, but the Presence of God.

Probably, the first to embrace life in this way will be the clergy. Some have already begun. They encourage the people they serve to come apart awhile.

COME APART AWHILE

The concluding portion of LIVING THE MYSTICAL LIFE TODAY is an invitation to COME APART AWHILE and to take one more step toward the simple life. As soon as possible arrange to spend three days alone in a secluded place. This invitation is not only to you, but to the Spirit of God within you to rise and assert Its power and dominion in your life. Jesus spent three days in the tomb before His resurrection, and it will take at least that long for the Christ in you to emerge from the tomb of your humanity.

When you are alone for three days, take nothing to read and do not listen to the radio or television. Instead, take a notebook and pen to jot down thoughts and experiences you have. Remember, the purpose of your pilgrimage is to experience God's presence. If you and I went to a secluded place in order to get to know one another, it would be rude of me to read while you were with me. Actually, my reading would be a way to avoid getting to know you. Therefore, no books and no distractions are permitted for three days.

AN INVITATION

The results of the pilgrimage are unpredictable aside from the realization that you are embracing the mystical life today. I would be interested in learning of your time alone and your joys and tribulations in living the mystical life today. I invite your letters and comments. I can be contacted at: jimrosemergy@gmail.com

THE SIMPLE LIFE

May the simple life awaken you from the slumber of human limitation, and may the world you awaken in be God's kingdom.

There the fields are white unto harvest, and the trees bear fruit in every season.

There will be a child finding joy in simple things and a mother bearing witness to the truth.

Be like the prophet who was fed by the ravens, and let God nourish you with His Presence.

Allow yourself to be led by the still waters, and listen for the wellspring rising up in you to eternal life.

And above all, be in the world, but not of it. Resist not and look for nothing to change.

Instead, come apart awhile and find the changeless within you waiting for you to wait.

THE SIMPLE LIFE

There is a rare life which has been lived by a few people who have walked the earth. These servants of God and humankind discovered the principles allowing one to live a life centered in God. They judged not by appearances and took no thought for what they were to eat, drink, or wear. They sought the kingdom and found God to be closer than hands and feet and breathing. If the promise of the rare and simple life has been given to you, *Living the Mystical Today* will guide you to a closer walk with God.

Jim Rosemergy's purpose is to assist humankind in its discovery of the new spirituality. For nearly 40 years, through the study of mystical works, prayer and meditation, he has explored the path that leads to spiritual awakening.

CPSIA information can be obtained
at www.ICGtesting.com
Printed in the USA
LVHW031614170521
687659LV00003B/818